NOWHERE

near

the

BOTTOM

Fred Bailey's Inspirational
Life Story and Philosophy

By Fred Bailey *with Susan White Newell*

This book is dedicated, first, to my parents, Ernest and Mattie Bailey. Their lives were just one step up from slavery, and they had to grin and bear a lot just so their kids could have a chance at life. From scrubbing floors in other people's homes to growing other people's crops, they gave all that they could and suffered much humiliation as a sacrifice for us.

Secondly, I dedicate this book to two younger sisters whom I never got to know. They didn't even get a chance at life due to our deprived circumstances. Both passed before they were even a year old.

Fred Bailey

"We're living just as a result of breathing, but life requires a journey. It requires you to *move*."

Fred Bailey

CONTENTS

FOREWORD

What does it mean to be "fully human," or to reach your *human potential?*

Fred Bailey lived the first decade of his life not knowing he was blind, never even suspecting that the contrasts of light and dark, and the ill-defined shapes that constituted his vision, were any different from what his brothers and sisters, mother and father, classmates and teachers, saw.

"I thought everybody had trouble going up and down steps, and seeing things," Fred recalls. "I didn't know that it was unique to me."

From the time he was three years old, Fred worked from sunup to sundown alongside twelve siblings in the tobacco fields of Middle Tennessee, sowing and harvesting, and in the woods picking berries and hauling wood, and on farms tending animals. For years, he managed to dodge the wrath of the alcoholic and abusive father he feared, but couldn't see.

At age 10, he was diagnosed with retinitis pigmentosa (RP), a rare inherited disease in which the light-sensitive retina of the eye progressively degenerates, resulting in complete blindness. He was sent away to board at the Tennessee School for the Blind and discovered an environment that was in such stark contrast to his life in the country, he said it might as well have been Egypt. Fred was among the first group of students to racially integrate the school, making his transition there that much more difficult. But he persevered and became a champion wrestler, winning against sighted competitors from around the state and ultimately vying for the state championship title.

When Fred graduated high school at age twenty-one, his vision was limited to daylight and darkness. But he went on to college, without a guide dog or even a cane.

To attend Tennessee State University, he memorized the turns and stops of the Jefferson Street public bus, sometimes discovering he had boarded the wrong bus and would need to get off, make his way back to the bus stop, and try again. He mentally cataloged the steps, turns, hallways, and doorways of campus buildings from one semester to the next, obtaining a college degree at the age of thirty-five. Along the way he married, worked for General Electric, owned his own business, volunteered and began raising a family— including biological, adopted, and foster children. In 2001, he started a nonprofit for kids who needed the same thing he had found: a way to defy the odds.

This is Fred Bailey's life: full of torment and scorn, hunger and cold, and prejudice in peculiar places. But that's not what this book is about.

This book is about discovering your human potential and what you are truly capable of when weaknesses are negated, when what's lacking is ignored, and when crutches and safety nets are disregarded. Because anything is possible when, in Fred's words, "Your character is set and there is dogged determination."

Susan White Newell

INTRODUCTION

Get Up and Get Moving

I am the envy of hundreds of thousands of people.

This blind, black man.

Why? Because I'm already in America, and all those people are still trying to get here.

We've got something as Americans and we don't realize what it is. We get a glimpse of what it is when terrorists come over here and use planes to bomb us. Or when we listen to the news and hear of people from Mexico and Cuba losing their lives trying to get here. But then we get complacent and go back to whining, and basically look at the country as if, "You need to do more for me. You need to give me more, you need to be more of this or more of that." But America has been all it's supposed to be to me. It took the environment that I came up in to realize that.

In America, you can do anything if you work hard and persevere. That's why people are dying to come here. *Literally*.

You don't need a level playing field to make it—to get the right start. You need two things: the rudiment of respect and a strong work ethic. Then you'll find that your blindness or deafness or blackness or whatever, is the least important part of you. You're going to find out that, only in America, can you truly rise above—if you keep the respect factor and work ethic in focus.

As I read history, I recognize that we'd like to think that our country was founded on religious freedom. But I think we were founded more on work ethic than anything. When you start clearing forests with axes and take picks to build roads and cabins, find food by hunting and gathering, *that's* work. And that's the way life was at the beginning of this country. We had great character back then.

When I look at individuals who I think made America great, they weren't so spiritual or religious—they were hard workers. *That* is the human condition. Human beings are designed and predisposed to hard work, because hard work does something for the character that church can't do and that school can't do. Once you put in a hard day's work and you can sit down at the end of the day and be tired from that, it does something for the human psyche.

As I came up through the ranks—hiding from my daddy, doing chores, being ridiculed at school—I realized that the good thing about America is that if you can hold it together, you're going to come out on the other side of that bad stuff. In most countries, the degradation is so severe, I don't know if you can come out on the other side. In countries like Syria, people are so deprived that the only way to make it is to totally escape the country.

So, if you were born on American soil, you're already a winner. You've got to have the wherewithal to accept that and take advantage of it. What is it that's clouding your vision? If there's something that's making you think you're on the bottom, you need to know that, as an American, you're nowhere near the bottom. You'd be on the bottom if you were in Iraq or Iran right now. You'd be on the bottom maybe if you were in Nigeria. But you're an American! You're nowhere near the bottom.

What is it that makes you think you're down? I want anyone who is faltering out there, who is thinking, "Gosh, if my father had just stayed in my life," or, "My momma just wasn't nice when I was growing up," I want you to pull yourself up through your own power. Don't waste your time whining, thinking that you're in this predicament because of where your mother or a bad teacher put you. Stop using your circumstances to define you, and use them to *prepare* you.

I'm not preaching or being sanctimonious—I'm just telling you that this is how I got to where I am. You can do it, too. Pick up this book and get moving.

Fred Bailey

CHAPTER ONE

Sulfur Water

We got our water from the spring, and even in the summertime it was good and cold. The spring came from a creek that ran through the woods. There was always watercress growing profusely in it that acted as a filter. We would lie on our stomachs and drink out of it, but you had to be really careful because snakes could get in it. Shoot, we drank with the coyotes. I guess there weren't any animals in those woods that we didn't know and that didn't know us.

But every now and then that spring would go dry. Then we would have to go down and get water from this sulfur water pump. You ever had any sulfur water? We had to drink it. It has great medicinal properties and it's better if you drink it cold, but we didn't have the luxury of getting it cold. We just needed water.

The pump was near the Summers' place, these people who lived down below us. And it was electric—you turned the faucet on and the water came out.

My brother Joe always went with me. He knew something was wrong with me and felt like he should look after me. Well, once when I was six or seven years old, I slipped on a rock and fell with the glass jug I was carrying. It about cut my hand off and it scared Joe to death. We never had a phone, so he ran to get my daddy.

I remember being in the house of the people who wrapped my hand up. I never came unglued. I have a high pain threshold and I take things in stride. I never believe that what happens to me can't be undone or is going to do me in. It's just something to be dealt with.

They must have called Uncle Carter, because he came and got me and took me to Meharry Hospital in Nashville. My sister went with us; she was 17 or 18 years old, and she told me that accident was her way out, her escape. She stayed in Nashville and never came back home. She never liked living in the country, and my daddy was rough.

I vaguely remember being in the hospital, but I don't remember how long. They sewed my hand back on. Two of my sisters still argue over who stayed in the hospital with me, but I don't remember either of them being there.

But I know my daddy would not have stayed. No, he would not have stayed.

CHAPTER TWO

You'd Better Be Blind

There were fifteen of us children, and it was almost like when people would say "the Baileys," it seems like they said it almost with venom in their voices or something. I don't know why.

We were always outside, always in the woods, most of our lives. It was beautiful in the summertime, but we were out there even in the wintertime when it was cold. We stayed in the woods to stay away from my father. When he was drunk, and that was most of the time, you just did not want to do anything to stir him up. We had a lot of chores in the woods anyway. We cut wood for heating and cooking; we had to fill the corner up in that old plank house so that we would have heat through the night, or my father would go completely off the deep end. And we had to get night water. We walked at least sixty yards to the spring, carrying buckets and jugs to get enough water to get us through the night, because there was no indoor plumbing. But we made sure everything was done.

And my momma was just like us. She was just doing everything she could to keep this man off of us and off of her, trying to keep herself out of the way of his lunacy. She was in survival mode. We were all just surviving in that hellhole back in the day.

We very seldom went to school because we lived so far away. The nearest neighbor was about a mile and a half from us and their house is where you had to go to catch the bus. To get there, you had to cross the creek and when it rained it was just terrible. My brothers and sisters could step on rocks and get across. But often, once we finally got across the creek, I'd have a shoe full of water because I missed the rocks. And then the dirt road where we would catch the bus would be muddy.

When we finally got to school, we got bullied like crazy. Not just from the kids, but from the teachers, too. We were always raggedy: our toes out of our shoes or wearing shoes that didn't have a bottom. We didn't have any lunch, we didn't have *anything*. I remember sometimes when we did get to school—this is before the time of free lunch—they wouldn't leave you in the classroom if you didn't have lunch—you had to go into the cafeteria where you stood along the wall while everybody else ate. I think once or twice the principal might have offered to buy us something. But we said no to even that. It was apparent that we were hungry, but we had too much pride to take it.

And we were the whipping boys of everybody else in the school because we never, *ever* fought back. My father just didn't go for that type of stuff. So, we took a lot of things from outside of the house, and we took a lot of things inside. It just kept you wondering all the time, "What'd I do?" You're out in the woods and you're wondering, "Where is the break going to come from?"

My break came while I was at Union Elementary. I was walking down the hall one day and I just plowed into a teacher of mine who was coming out of the classroom. I never saw her. I mean, just as soon as I got there, she came out. This was around 1963 or 1964, and I was nine or 10 years old. Back then, the teachers would literally just beat you to death. Most of the teachers in that school had a paddle *and* a strap and were quick to use both of them. They just beat the nonsense out of you. And that woman had me by the collar and was marching me down to the office when she said, "Boy, you'd either better be blind or else."

That was the first time that term ever came across my mind. *Blind.* The first time I ever heard it. I didn't know what she was talking about. I remember her taking me down to the principal, B.J. Hall. We called him "Fessor Hall." I remember him saying, "What's wrong with you, boy?" And man, I was shaking. His wife was sort of like the guidance counselor, and I remember she took me to a doctor down in Nashville. I was scared to death. We didn't say anything going down the road; she didn't say anything to me, and I didn't say anything to her.

I remember winding up in this chair, sitting there, timid and scared. And I remember this doctor, sitting at his desk. I could hear him shuffling his papers, and he says, "ummmmm." And he put them down. He just grunted. Then he said, "Son, you've got a problem that we're just now learning about. It's called retinitis pigmentosa."

Well, I couldn't spell anything but like pig, dog, cow. Shoot, that thing sounded like it had thirty letters in it. And I thought to myself, *What in the world is he talking about?* But then I thought about that teacher, Miss Hayes, and boy, she told me I'd better be blind. So, I timidly asked the doctor, "Sir, does that mean that I'm blind?" And I could tell he didn't want to hurt my feelings. Then he said, "Yes, son. For all practical purposes, you're blind." And I said, "Thank God." I'm sure he thought I was crazy.

When I went back to school, Miss Hayes was waiting on me. She asked me, "What's wrong with you, boy?" And I said, "I'm blind." She just spun on her heels and walked away.

CHAPTER THREE

I Never Saw Anything to Fear

I was born on this lady's farm, in Gallatin, Tennessee, in 1953. Of course, I don't remember it, but that's what my momma told me. I wasn't born in a hospital. I never went to a hospital until I almost cut off my hand on the glass jug.

My parents were sharecroppers, and I was born the tenth down, so there were already a number of kids ahead of me. William Ernest, Bobby Gene, Elizabeth Ann, Charles Wayne, Jerry Dowell, Charlie Woodard, Nina Kay, Joe Lindale, Sharon Linette, then me, Freddy Davis. Then there was Ruth Marie, Joyce Glynn, Mary Alice, Judy Carol, and Margaret Lee.

I lost two younger sisters early. I don't know how they died. Older people didn't talk about things like that back then. I always guessed from pneumonia because that frame house was always so cold. We had moved there when I was about two, and around October—sometimes even in early September—it would start getting cool. We used to walk around and take rags and paper and anything else we could find to stuff the holes between the planks and around the windows where the cold air was going to come through because there wasn't any insulation. I can't remember if the windows were broken, but if they were, we stuffed rags in those, too. My brothers probably could see the light where the holes were, but I would just plug wherever I could feel air. If we didn't get all the holes plugged just right, we were cold, even with the stove going. And I'm thinking those two babies caught pneumonia. They had to be just months old, not even a year. It was such a deprived life.

I don't know how many acres this house was on, but there was land as far as you could see. You rarely saw people. We were stuck back there by ourselves. It was probably dangerous. We were with coyotes, foxes, porcupines, and skunks, among other things. But I learned a lot from the animals back on the farm. I paid close attention to them—when they got quiet, or even when they made noises, that meant something was around. When I'd hear animals chirping rapidly and scurrying away, I took my cues from them. Often, predators sense fear and will attack, but I couldn't see anything, so I never acted afraid. It's hard to tell how many animals I came into close proximity with that never hurt me.

The house had a tin roof. We always used to throw a ball up on top of it and let it roll off. And it had a long front porch—my mother always loved long front porches. All houses back then had chimneys because you heated the house with a wood-burning stove. There were only four rooms: a living room with the stove, a kitchen, my momma and daddy's bedroom, and one bedroom for the rest of us. In the summertime we slept on the floor or on the porch. But the house got cold in the winter. It was wired for electricity, but we didn't pay for it. Instead, I remember using a wood stove and a kerosene lamp. We slept in our clothes a lot under these big quilts, three to a bed, two at the head and one at the foot. Come morning, my father wanted that fire made before he got up and it was left up to Joe to get it started. When Joe would get up, I would get up. Shoot, I was *glad* to get up because the bed was so full; everybody tried to ball up in a knot to make room, but I'd been kicked so many times, and sometimes I was kicked right out of bed and ended up on the floor.

If it was the weekend, we washed our clothes—took them off, put on some clothes just as raggedy as the ones we took off, and washed them with our hands and hung them up. We only had two sets of clothes. We'd wear one to school for two to three days and then wash it out. You just washed and wore, washed and wore. Then we went and did what we had to do on the farm. There wasn't any breakfast.

My mother worked in people's homes. She'd do their cooking and cleaning and ironing. People all over Sumner County knew my mother because she worked for just about everybody. She didn't earn money. All she got was leftover food to feed us with sometimes. Leftover biscuits and bread, that type of thing. I'm not exactly sure how she felt about it because she never complained; she never seemed to be mad about it. She was not bitter. Even when she came home with no food, she never said, "I'm never going back—I hate this job." And the farm owners just didn't care. It wasn't like they said, "We're not going to pay Miss Mattie today." There were just no consequences. They knew she wasn't going to quit. She went back because she might get leftover food, and at least we ate those days.

I learned a lot from watching her do that. In this life you have to grin and bear some things. It's just as simple as that. And that's what she did; she grinned and bore *a lot* so that we would have a chance. Not that she was right, not that she was a martyr. She did whatever it took for her kids to survive. My mother wasn't the hugging, petting, kissing, nurturing type, but you watched what she did and you knew she was doing it for you. She sacrificed her dignity, pride, and so much more so that I might have a chance at life. She was the first person to show me how to make it in the world.

And all the kids who were old enough to walk worked on farms just so we would have a place to live; and that's what we got out of it: a roof over our heads. We milked the cows and went and got the baby calves at four o'clock in the morning and had to take care of them. We took care of the chickens. We planted the tobacco slips—that's what they called them—in early spring. Then in the summertime, we had to go out and cut tobacco and spike it on these sticks, and then you'd load them on a truck and take them to a barn and hang them. And I *hated* it because it was always hot and I couldn't see the snakes that liked to be around in there. I never knew to run until everybody else started running.

Then we had to get the wood in at night; go into the woods, cut down trees, drag them back up to the house and cut them up, and then we stacked it inside the house next to the stove. You had to have the wood in, and kindling in to get the wood started. The water we carried from the spring was for bathing, washing dishes, drinking … all of that. We'd heat the water on the stove and fill up this metal tub that was out there on the back porch, and you took your bath out there. But don't think we took a bath that often, because we didn't! It took so much water to fill this thing up and that thing up.

It was hard work, and my daddy was a taskmaster. We were staying on these farms by means of his agreeing to work them, only he didn't do a lot, he made us to do it. He drove the machinery, the use of a tractor or a plow; he did handle that because we were too young. But we never saw any money to buy food or groceries or anything from the work that we did. If the farm owner shared the meat when they killed hogs, my daddy would sell it. And we would never see his part of the tobacco crops that we were supposed to share. If he made any money, he drank it up. He would head straight to town and we knew where he was going and how he would be when he got back.

When my Daddy wasn't drunk, which wasn't often, he wouldn't say anything. He'd lie on the couch and that was it. When he was drunk, nothing seemed to be right. I don't know what he was searching for. Maybe he was looking for something or trying to mask something. I could never figure him out. I don't know whether he was mean or whether the alcohol was driving it. I'm thinking it was the alcohol because when he was sober, he was quiet.

So, growing up, we didn't eat well. Sometimes we didn't eat at all. Often, we dug for food at the trash dump. It was about two miles from where we lived, and we'd listen for the truck coming to the dump so we could run up there and go through the trash. We got anything that wasn't chewed to death. We dug for food, shoes, clothes, parts to build a bicycle, anything we could find.

Sometimes, we could eat when my brother and I found glass bottles along Route 109. We took the bottles up to a store called Mr. Down's to get the deposit. We would use the money to buy a bag of pinto beans or bologna. But that didn't go far for a bunch of kids, especially a bunch of kids who didn't get to eat on a regular basis.

In the summertime, we could do a little better because things always grew. There was plenty of fruit and nuts. We used to pick a lot of blackberries for the people who liked them but who didn't want to get stuck by chiggers and thorns, or deal with the snakes. We'd pick five-gallon buckets and sell them along the main highway for a dollar apiece. We also had plum trees, pear trees, and walnut trees, so we ate plenty of walnuts, hickory nuts, and persimmons. My family probably never suffered from scurvy because we got all the vitamin C we wanted!

But we were always hungry. Hungry *all* of the time. You know nowadays, when someone goes to the store, you hear the grocery bags when they're coming in. But I don't ever remember hearing bags in that house like someone was coming from a store. I don't remember *EVER* hearing bags. Or knowing of groceries on the table or anything like that.

CHAPTER FOUR

A Caste System

I always felt kind of different. I stayed out of everybody's way. And I think everybody just thought, "He's slow," or, "Something's wrong. He's mentally challenged." Because we didn't know what blind was.

After I was diagnosed with RP, they tested my siblings and discovered that two of my sisters and a brother also had it. It affects everybody differently. My sight was impacted right away, but my brother didn't have problems until he was about 39 years old. But neither my mother nor my father ever mentioned the word blind. I don't know why. My father probably just didn't care, and my mother probably didn't know what to say. But they never said the word blind. I never heard the term. I thought everybody had trouble going up and down steps and seeing things. I didn't know that it was unique to me.

We rarely went to school. Out of 180 days, we might have made 60 or 80. I got all the way through the third grade without them knowing I was blind! I remember reading *Dick and Jane* and I really couldn't see it, so I memorized it. "See Jane Run," and "Run, Spot, Run"; once you hear that a few times, it just sticks in your head. Teachers would write on the board and they would say, "Bailey, spell that." And I would say, "I don't know how." I didn't really mean, "I don't know how," but I didn't know to say that I couldn't *see* it.

After I saw the doctor in Nashville, the teacher tried these big thick glasses on me. Kids were so mean about those glasses. This one boy was unmerciful. Every day he and his friends would say, "Blind Freddy Bailey, blind Freddy Bailey!" A couple of times we'd go wrestling around in the hall. But somehow, I learned to use psychology early, because I wasn't a fighter. If I fought and it got back to my daddy, he'd kill me. So, I went to school one day, and he did the same thing he always did. He walked up calling me Blind Fred Bailey. I said, "You know Joe, I *am* blind, and I hope it never happens to you." And he never bothered me again. I never had any problem with him after that.

Everybody in that school treated us badly. It wasn't a race issue—everybody there was black. It was poverty. There was a hierarchy within the black community at that time. Depending on what church you went to, you were treated differently. You were treated differently if you were light-skinned or dark-skinned. You were bullied if they knew something about your parents, like, "The Baileys' daddy is a drunk." Or if you didn't have good clothes, hadn't had a bath, your hair wasn't combed, or you didn't have parents who would come to the school to advocate for you, the teachers treated you differently. This is what people don't understand: there is often prejudice within a race. It's almost like a caste system, within *every* race. When I was growing up, I was always embarrassed and ashamed, though being poor wasn't my fault.

So, we were glad to miss school. Half the time when we missed the bus, it was because we wanted to. We just weren't in the mood to be lectured all day. We were hungry. We knew we'd be humiliated during lunch. Then we'd have to go back to class where the teacher would hold us in disdain and the kids would be picking on us. Then we'd go home and have all these chores to do.

We didn't have the luxury of going off somewhere and licking our wounds, because all of these chores had to get done. That was my life.

Running into that teacher and getting sent to the school for the blind was probably the best thing that ever happened to me.

But I didn't want to go.

CHAPTER FIVE

We Have a School for People Like You

If I was standing nearly touching my mother, I could almost make out what she looked like. But I never could see in any detail. And even the ability to make out something when I was close-up touching somebody went away when I was 12 or 13. After that, if my mother was hugging me, I couldn't make out who she was except for her voice. Now, I can only tell people apart by the sound of their voices. There's nothing there. It's dark. But I grew up never knowing that as a limitation, so I don't know what it means to be blind.

It was about a year after my diagnosis that I remember a lady coming to our house and saying, "We have a school for people like you." Well, I had never been away from home in my life. And as bad as home was, it was still all I knew. But my mother said, "You're going." My two sisters with RP were going to go, too.

I told my brothers and sisters I didn't want to go. And one of my older brothers who quit school during fourth grade, said, "You know you don't have anything going here." I remember him saying, "You might try it, because I'm leaving." It was around 1964 and he was on his way to Detroit because one of my brothers who was in the military had settled there. So, my sisters and I moved to the Tennessee School for the Blind.

We didn't have any clothes to go there, and I don't know where the clothes came from. But somehow, some new clothes showed up. I don't know if we carried them in a bag or had suitcases or what. I don't think my daddy took us. I think it was my sister-in-law and my brother, with my mom and my two younger sisters.

The school was in Donelson, Tennessee, which was about thirty-five miles from the farm, but it felt like I was in Egypt. It was that stark of a difference. Other than the elementary school I went to, that was the first time that I had ever experienced a brick building. I'm not even sure if Union Elementary had a sidewalk or not, but you walked on a sidewalk everywhere you went at the new school. I stayed in a dorm with a bunch of people. And I was used to a bunch of people, but here I had a bed to myself. This place had a swimming pool, a water fountain, and a clinic. It was almost like living in a different century. There were three meals a day at a table with plates and forks and spoons.

The first thing we did when we got there was register for classes. They had so many kids because this was the first year that they were integrating. Before 1964, the schools were segregated and the blind black people used to go to a school on Hermitage Avenue in Nashville. I remember thinking to myself, *Of all the places to be segregated, why the blind schools?* At this integrated school, I got called all kinds of names by the students and by some of the staff. It was the first time that I had ever personally been called "nigger." I thought it was strange because we were at a blind school! It was by another student, and I knew what it meant, but it didn't bother me any. It truly didn't. I'd been through so much—it didn't have weight or power because of everything else that I had already gone through.

Back on the farm, I had become aware of the concept of "staying in your place." I noticed that we were always taught to say, "Yes sir," and "No sir," to anybody that was older than we were and to any white person, and we *definitely* had to say it to the people on whose farm we were living. This family that owned the farm had one son. The father was named Billy and the son was Bill, whom they called Little Bill. We would be walking, getting ready to go to the barn, my mother and father and some of the kids, and I remember distinctly that Little Bill would never call my mother and father Mr. and Mrs. Bailey. It was always, "Ernest" and "Mattie." But if we had called his daddy "Billy," our daddy would have knocked us down. As I got older, I realized that racism is a learned thing. I understood that when you're racist, something's wrong with you. There's a sheer lunacy to not liking somebody without knowing anything about them besides the color of their skin. My momma always said, "If people treat you well, you treat them well back. If they don't treat you well, you stay away from them." We were always taught, "You push *by* these people. You push *through* these people who won't give you a job, you push through those that won't let you rent here, that won't sell you a car there. You push through it."

My momma always told me, "Son, there's going to be people who say things about you because you're black, and people who say things about you because you're blind. Just know that people who try to demean you are fools; you're as good as anybody. But let me say this to you, I may not live long enough to see it, but make sure you get an education, because you're going to need it." I think that's why she insisted that I go to the school for the blind.

The kids there were from all over Tennessee. I can't remember how many were on campus that first year, but it was over two hundred. They had so many students that they used the gym as a dorm, and the dormitory supervisors had the wrestling room as their quarters. My bed was in the gym, and I basically never slept. Some of the students would get up and go to the bathroom in the night and come back and bump into your bed. I might doze off but then I snapped back awake. I probably wasn't really sleeping until I got into a proper dorm the next year where it was two to a room.

Some of the teachers at the school were mean just for the sake of being mean. It seemed like they had been hired from anywhere. My dormitory supervisor had burned down a truck stop. The school didn't even make us aware—*she* told us! We had some teachers that weren't all that educated. Some were downright racist. I remember one time, this teacher was pushing the desks together and this black child's fingers were there. She smashed the student's fingers between the desks. The child screamed, and the teacher said, "Well, you should have moved them." And then we had some teachers that I thought were mean when I was in school, but I later learned to appreciate them because I realized they wanted me to do well and they were just tough. That was exactly what I needed. Some of my teachers were great teachers. I still talk to a lot of those people today and tell them how much I appreciate them.

Some of the students didn't like the black kids being there either. A lot of that changed as time went on. I think it was just the newness of the thing. Some of these white kids came from further back in the woods than I did where they never saw anybody except who was in their house. But we were familiar with white people. We lived on white people's farms, so we saw them often enough to know how to deal with them. We didn't have a problem with the race thing, we didn't have a problem with them liking us or not liking us. We were indifferent. I had gone through the fire—and came out the other side of it. I was ready to take whatever was thrown at me.

We were on a schedule. We would go to breakfast at seven thirty. We'd sit at this table that sat eight or 10. There were real plates and servers. All of the food was brought out to the tables in bowls that we learned how to serve ourselves out of and then pass around the table. If you ran out of something, you would hold the bowl or plate up and someone would come replace it. There was plenty of food, so we ate well.

We had breakfast from seven-thirty to eight o'clock, then we went back to our dorms, brushed our teeth, and went to class. We had to be at school at eight-thirty. We had English, math, science, history, geography, study hall, and co-op—which is where you prepare to interview for jobs or can work part of the day at a job. Lunch was at noon and we finished school at three twenty-five. Then we went to our dorms and studied, or we went outside and played basketball or whatever you wanted to play. Dinner was from five to five-thirty, and then we went back to our dorms and played a little more. Then we went to study hall from six to eight. We would come down to this big rec room that had a lot of tables and that's where we sat and did our homework. The campus was shut down, completely quiet. If we had to go to the library, we'd get a pass. Then from eight to ten it was free time. We socialized, talked to friends, or watched TV. Ten o'clock it was lights out. Our days were pretty regimented.

I learned Braille at the school for the blind, but we had to learn to write. They wouldn't let us sign our names with an x. We learned tactilely—what the letters felt like.

I can still write a note to you that you could probably read.

CHAPTER SIX

Do Not Hyphenate Me

When I first went to the school for the blind, they had a wrestling team, but I didn't know anything about wrestling. My dorm was taking up the gym so the team would practice in the gym lobby or on the stage in the auditorium, and I got to understand a little of what it was about. It was a tradition there that the varsity wrestling team put pee-wee teams together amongst the younger students—that's how they got their wrestlers and built their team. So after my first year there, I was on one of those pee-wee teams. I weighed eighty-five pounds.

That was the second time I was called "nigger," this time by one of the wrestling coaches. I was working out with one of the other wrestlers and I guess that coach didn't like the way I was handling him. I remember the coach saying, "Get out of the way, I'm going to kill this nigger." Well, that coach wasn't that much better than me, and he had a hard time killing this nigger. I knew what I was doing—I was a country boy.

Come tournament time, I wrestled two Harris's. One was John Michael Harris and the other was John Lee Harris. John Lee is now the director of handicap services at Middle Tennessee State University. We're still friends to this day. I beat John Michael and John Lee and I won my tournament. I suppose I got a trophy, I don't remember. But that was the first time that I realized, "I *am* somebody. I *can* do something. I'm a champion, I won this tournament. *I* did that." I think I started to come into myself then. Ralph Brewer, who was the head wrestling coach, came over there and said, "I want to see you on the varsity team Monday." I was only 85 pounds, and I said to myself, *I'm not going over there!*

The next Monday, I was just playing with my friends and talking when Coach Brewer sends the heavyweight and the 189-pounder over to get me. Back then, there was no limit on the heavyweight class. Ours was six-two or six-three and weighed 375 pounds. They came and got me in my dorm and took me over to the gym to wrestling practice. I got over there and they thrust this sweat suit in my arms and said, "Go put that on." I was scared to death. I changed and put this thing on, and I came back and I was walking slowly to the gym. I got into the wrestling room and the heat hits me in the face. And everybody has been practicing and they're all wet; it's so hot and they're so sweaty.

I was only 85 pounds, but the lowest weight class at the time was the 98-pound class, which was the class I was going to represent. So, I had to work out with the next weight class up, which was the 112-pound, and my partner threw me around like it was nothing. That first year I remember getting pinned so fast that when the whistle blew I thought they were blowing it to *start* the match—I didn't realize it was over! But the second year, I won my NIL (Nashville Interscholastic League) weight class and my district. I finally started wrestling and I give Coach Brewer a lot of credit. He was no-nonsense, tough; just hardcore. But I was used to it because my father was that way. Brewer was that way in terms of work ethic and in terms of discipline, in a way that said, "I'm going to pull everything out of you that you've got." He was tough like that, but not in a punishing way.

Wrestling is what brought me to where I am now. I started winning, and I began to realize that the younger kids seemed to kind of idolize me. I started to do fairly well in school and to understand what it meant to have honor, to have someone look up to you. What it meant to be something and *what it meant to have gotten there on your own.* What it meant to come through the deprivation that I had come through and now here I was with people shaking my hand because I had done something well.

I could look back and say that, in a way, my father did a good thing for me by depriving me. He tried to strip me of anything and everything that would make me proud or confident or whole, but I was able to overcome that and not let it hold me back. Things were so bad when I was growing up, but I don't think that I could have gotten to this point had I not had to persevere through those hard times. I had learned what it meant to survive, to embrace a strong work ethic and respect for others, and to use that to make it on my own.

I truly understand what it really means to be an American.

At the beginning of all our matches, they played the national anthem. Everybody would stand, and then the announcers would introduce the wrestlers. They would say "At the 98-pound weight class, for the Tennessee School for the Blind: Fred Bailey." Then I'd walk to the edge of the mat and stand until all the team was called, and then they'd introduce the visiting team.

You had a few seconds to reflect when you walked up to the edge of that mat. I didn't think about my opponent. I was always thinking, "It is *so* great to be an American. I *am* an American and I realize what it means to be one. And I want all the individuals that have gone before me to know that I realize."

I was thinking about the World War II veterans. If you could ever say a war made sense, it was *that* war. I also thought about the people in the civil rights movement. They took a lot and gave up a lot. The verbal slander and the kickings and the beatings and the jailings and the lynchings—the whole mix. These people paid the ultimate price for me to be the best American that I could be. So every time I took to the wrestling mat, every time they played that national anthem, I thought about all of these people.

I am a black man taking this mat here in a minute. Are you proud of me? Am I making you proud of me? I'm clean cut. I'm going to pin this guy, but I'm not going to be demeaning. I'm going to shake hands and be a gentleman all the way through this whole thing. Do you know that the humiliation that you suffered is being taken to heart? Do you understand that all that you have sacrificed has not been in vain? Thank you for what you've done. This is the only way I know to pay you back. I'm hoping it's worthy of what you've done. I hope you're proud of me. I hope I'm living up to what you want me to do, after all that you've gone through.

This was the 1960s—a time of turmoil. Martin Luther King, Jr. was coming into his own. You know the music back at that time was James Brown, "Say It Loud—I'm Black and I'm Proud." And I was in the middle of all of this racism and prejudice stuff.

I remember one time, one of the black supervisors at the school went into a diabetic coma on the porch, and they called this ambulance from one of the nearby funeral homes. But the funeral home replied, "We don't pick up blacks." So they had to call Holmes Funeral Home to come and pick this lady up. And she just lay there until they finally came. I have never forgotten what all the civil rights people went through so that kind of stuff would not happen today, so that a lady like that could be treated with some dignity.

So while I was standing there at the edge of that mat waiting for them to make the introductions and waiting to meet my opponent, you don't know how proud I was to be an American. Not an *African-*American, an *American*. Nothing … not calling me names, not my father and his alcoholism, not denying me food at school, not segregation, not Jim Crow, *nothing* could take that away from me. Everything that I had gone through … getting on the wrestling team, achieving these awards, and realizing how many kids were looking up to me as a hero, realizing that now I was representing the Tennessee School for the Blind, all of that just made me feel that regardless of what anybody thought about me, I was a *full-blooded American*. Look where I came from, look what I did. That's why I will not be called an African-American today. Do not hyphenate me. I realize that there are a lot of people who have gone and lost their lives for me to be a *full* American.

I often wonder, why do some people prefer to be called African-American? I think it is because they are not real confident in their own identity. They will tell you that they are. They'll say, "No, no, Africa is my heritage. We were taken out of our country and brought to a land that we had no familiarity with, no affinity for. We were taken away from our ancestors."

All of that may be true, but it does not make *you* any of that. You are an American whether you want to be or not. The reason that you call yourself an African-American is because there are those in this country who have made you feel so diminished that you're trying to take on another persona.

You have no relationship with Africa at all. You may visit Africa, and you may like it. But I can assure you that you're not going to stay there. You have only taken on that mantle because someone has made you feel bad about your real skin. Someone has made you feel like you're not an American, and you've bought into it.

Well, I don't have to prove anything to anybody, white supremacist or NAACP. I was born in 1953 on American soil. My whole life has been spent in America. To try to link me to my ancestry is looking backward, and my head will not swivel. I can only go forward.

Where I've come from is nowhere near as important as where I am now and where I'm going, because I'm never going backward.

So my pride and dignity will not allow you to hyphenate me or let you try to reduce me to what you want me to be. If you try to call me an African-American, it's ludicrous. I do not feel African, I feel American. There may be some people in this country that don't think I should be here, but even those people know that I can no more change my color than they can change theirs. This is a God thing. You would have to talk to God about that. You can hate me all you want, you can even kill me—but you've just killed an American. It's as simple as that. I'm a full-blooded American.

The trick is to realize that, as an American, you are already a winner. Now, how do you take advantage of that? You take advantage of that by getting an education, having a work ethic, and teaching those individuals who, for whatever reason, have been told that black is bad, black will never amount to anything, black is not intelligent, black is not civilized, that they can break that.

My parents raised me as a black male, not as an African-American. They raised me as a whole person, not a blind person. If you can't feel good about who you really are, then you're living a lie.

You Can Go a Little Bit Further Tomorrow

Ralph Brewer was a student at the Tennessee School for the Blind from 1954–1962. His senior year he won the state title in wrestling for his weight class. He returned to TSB to become the wrestling coach in 1965. These are his recollections of the time he spent with Fred Bailey.

I got involved with Freddy in a program we called Pee Wee wrestling.

At the end of the wrestling season, we would have the smaller kids come out to participate, and the varsity kids would divide up and coach them. Freddy was involved in that, and I saw immediately that he had some athletic ability. He came through that program and started wrestling at a very young age on the varsity team. He was an outstanding little athlete. Very easy to coach; he would do anything I would tell him to do.

The School for the Blind team was famous in Nashville. We would work with all of these schools around town to get them started in the sport. We were in the Nashville Interscholastic League, and we won a lot of tournaments. Our team didn't wrestle other blind schools, only public schools. My senior year when I won the state title, our team came in second in the state behind Baylor in Chattanooga.

At our high school we had, I'd say, twenty-five boys. And out of that number, not that many were interested in wrestling. We had so few athletes, and we had to compensate for that by working hard. We practiced at night, on Saturdays and Sundays; it was a seven-day-a-week thing. As a coach, I approached it with the attitude that if we were going to be successful, with the limitations we had, then we had to be in better shape, have more knowledge, and execute better than our competition. That's where the time comes in.

Of all the senses we have, vision is the unifying sense; it's the one that ties our world together for us. A sighted person can just scan around the room and pick up so much information. But the blind person without that visual input, they don't get it. So you have to develop a program or system where you do hands-on. I couldn't just flash a filmstrip up and say, "Hey, on your takedown you're going to do this. Watch this guy and see how you do it."

Instead, with the kids who were congenitally blind, I had to start by physically placing my hand on their foot and showing them, "*This* is where you set your foot. When the whistle blows, you put your foot *here*, you put it out like *this* and this is how your arm goes"—because they had no concept! And it was just *so hard*. It just takes so much time to do that. And that's the reason we were over there till nine o'clock at night and on Saturdays and Sundays. We worked HARD. *They* worked hard. Plain old hard work, and time and effort.

But after these kids learn they can do that—it's a life-altering thing.

You see, one of the things that blind and visually-impaired people have is a lack of self-esteem. It certainly was the case with me. Society doesn't expect a whole lot out of blind people, doesn't expect them to be productive. The general attitude is that they are hopeless and helpless, to be cared for and taken care of.

Let me give you an example. A mother takes her little blind baby into the grocery store and puts the baby in the cart. As people pass by, someone might say, "Excuse me, is your baby blind?" And the mother replies "Yes," he or she is. "Oh, I'm so sorry," the person says. And this baby is hearing all of that, and they grow up with this: "When people meet me, they feel sad about my circumstances." That engenders in blind children an inferiority complex.

You have to break that. The way I tried to break that with the kids I coached is to ever-increase the challenges. "If you go this far today, you can go a little bit further tomorrow." And you take them further than they think they can go, and when they get there, they say, "Gosh, I can do this." Keep increasing the level of expectation. Wrestling is one of those sports that can provide an individual with self-esteem and with the realization that, "I *can* achieve. I *can* be somebody." I've seen it happen so many times before, and it turns your life around—makes you believe in yourself.

I could go back and look at the kids who wrestled when I was a student at the Tennessee School for the Blind, and look at the ones from Freddy's era—the ones that I coached—and almost every one of them is successful in life. You have to have discipline in anything that you go into in life; if you have no discipline, then the first thing that's going to happen when you run into opposition or an obstacle—when things get tough—you're going to quit.

But after TSB, when you come up to a challenge in life, you look back and compare it to what you achieved in wrestling—because it required so much discipline and hard work. Even as a seventy-five-year-old man, I still make that comparison today: "If I could do *that*, then I can do *this*, because this is not anywhere as difficult as that." It has a carry-over value; I think that's what wrestling did for me and Freddy and the other kids.

You know, a lack of self-esteem manifests differently. For a blind person, it manifests itself by withdrawal and sitting. In the sighted, it manifests itself in cockiness, in the sagging-and-dragging, "I want to get attention" type of thing. But it's the same basic problem, I think. And here I go playing amateur psychologist ... but I think it is a lack of self-esteem and a lack of expectation that you have to overcome, the "I'll just sit and draw my welfare check, and everything will be fine."

Kids without self-esteem don't have any expectations, so you have to give them some.

CHAPTER SEVEN

I Just Trailed Their Voices

I saw my sisters only in passing. Their dorm was across the campus from mine. But I knew that, like me, they were growing in confidence and establishing relationships.

Once all of the students got to know each other, black and white, we became very close, because we were out there nine months out of the year almost. Some of the boys I met at that school became almost like brothers to me.

When I left home at age eleven, I never went back to live there. I sometimes saw my momma at the holidays, usually only once or twice a year. I didn't always come home for Thanksgiving because they didn't shut the school down. Sometimes, I didn't come home for Christmas because I was on the wrestling team and we had tournaments, so I would go home with a friend. In the summer, I'd try to get a job in Nashville so I would stay with my older sister or my uncle. But when I did see my momma, she could tell that I was growing up and doing well, and the decision she'd made was the right one. And when I started working, I bought her a phone so that I could call.

I had two jobs in school. I used to work for the Neighborhood Youth Corps (NYC), and that's how I bought my clothes for school. I helped to clean up schools during the summer and get them ready for the fall. I was assigned to Isaac Litton High School in Nashville. I think I made about fifty dollars a week. I was fifteen or sixteen years old at this point, and I'd use my money to buy shirts, pants, shoes—the things I needed to get ready to go to school.

Before I worked for the Neighborhood Youth Corps, I went and stayed with my oldest sister in Nashville. She worked for a company that built airplane wings. I kept my nieces and nephew while she went to work. They loved me to death, and they were good kids. All three of the girls would read to me, so they got a head start on reading. In return for my watching them, my sister helped me get school clothes. But we were late getting them. Because I didn't have clothes to wear to school, I didn't go until two weeks after the school year started. The people at school thought that I had dropped out. The principal saw me and said, "Freddy, where you been?" And I said, "Well, I had to wait until I got some clothes." And he said, "We would have gotten you some clothes!" And I thought, *You ought to know me well enough by now to know that I'd be too embarrassed.* It was embarrassing to me just to have him say that. We were extremely poor and I think from time to time they did give us clothes, but it was always embarrassing. When I started working at the NYC, I was able to buy my clothes. I worked there for two summers.

Then I got a job bagging groceries at an H.G. Hills grocery store that was near the school. It was for co-op my junior and senior year, which trained you on how to apply for jobs, how to interview, and how to be a good employee. So I walked to the store and talked to the manager. They had never hired a blind person before me. I persuaded them that I could do the job. I said, "Give me two weeks, and if I can't do it, you don't even have to pay me for those two weeks."

How did I bag groceries and get them to their cars? Well, the customers didn't know I was blind because I had coping skills. Usually, the people were in front of you as you took their groceries to the car, so I would just keep them talking and would just follow their voices. I was always lagging behind because I was trailing their voices, but I could always find my way *back* to the store because I could hear all the noise inside.

CHAPTER EIGHT

I've Done What I Came Here to Do

When I got to the age where I realized what my mother was going through, I said to myself, *I will never disappoint this woman. I will do everything in my power to make her proud of something or somebody.* I was going to get through school and get that high school diploma even if it killed me, even if I was 80 years old when I finished. I lived to make her proud. I remember that the spring before graduation, I started feeling *so* good about achieving that. I was thinking, *I'm going to get a high school diploma that I earned.*

I wasn't the smartest person in the school. I wasn't even the smartest person in the class. But, I worked hard enough to get a diploma. I was the first person in my family to get one, and I wanted my mother to be the first one to see it. She didn't come to the school very often, but she made it to my graduation. I think that my youngest sister had just started driving and drove momma to the school. My nephew, Ricky, and my other two sisters who went to the school for the blind were there, too.

The staff at the school served a meal at our regular meal time. It was nice, but I can't even remember what we had. But, I remember my mother. That was the one time that I saw her with a lot of pride. She smiled and she took that diploma and she was just holding on to it. I knew it because everybody was telling me, "Your mother's happy as she can be." Some of the cooks said to me, "Your mother is a happy woman." And she should have been, because she had not had many opportunities to be happy.

There were a lot of emotions that day. I remember my mom saying, "I'm proud of you." And I knew she was, but I was more proud than she was because I had made *her* proud.

I remember putting on the cap and gown and thinking, *This is the first time I've ever had to hold my head this straight.* We went up on the stage and I kept thinking that the hat was going to topple off of my head. It didn't take much to embarrass me. If that thing had fallen off my head, I would have wanted to crawl under a chair and hide. We went up on the stage and I remember a girl in my class, Debra Gilreap, was crying and saying how much she was going to miss all of us and so forth. And I remember telling her, "Shut up, I'm glad to get out! I'm going to miss you all, too, but I've done what I came here to do. I'm ready to go."

For many of us, graduation meant that we were going to be on our own for the first time. David Hubbard, Terry Alton, myself and, I think it was John Harris, we were going to rent rooms together. We were great buddies; we had already lived together for almost ten years. Terry and David were white and John was black. We had the dormitory supervisor looking in the paper for places to live, and she said, "Wait a second, here's a house that's renting rooms." The house was in East Nashville. I called, and when the lady answered the phone, I said, "Yes ma'am, I'm calling about the room you have to rent." The first thing out of her mouth was, "Are you colored?" and I said, "Yes, ma'am." And she said, "We don't rent to coloreds."

This was in the mid-1970s. That's the kind of stuff we went through. We realized we weren't going to be able to live together. So Terry and David went back home to their hometowns, and John got a job in Nashville.

I had people tell me they'd go to apply for jobs and hear, "We don't hire black people here." For me, it was, "We've never hired a blind person before." That's what they'd say, and pretty much shut the door. So if I had been someone who gives up easily, I would have been out of luck. But we Baileys, we're not wired that way. We just keep on pushing and keep knocking until someone says, "Yes, we have a place to rent," or, "I will hire you." That's the way we've always been. That's the way I still am today.

I remember thinking when I graduated that I had been living at the school with those people for ten years or more and we had become brothers, black and white. I thought, *Man, it's all going to change.* But I had achieved that monumental thing for me, and I knew then that I wasn't through. It was time to go to work. Let's keep pushing.

CHAPTER NINE

I Didn't Know to Be Scared

After I graduated from the school for the blind, I didn't want to go to college. I was sick of school. All I wanted to do was work.

When I was growing up in the '60s, if you could get hired at GE or DuPont, you were there for life. That's all I wanted. But I was working at Auto Mart in inventory control—unloading trucks and stocking shelves—and it didn't pay a lot. Everybody was telling me, "You need to go on to school," so I did. There was an organization, Service for the Blind, I think, that helped me get into college, but when I started making good grades, another organization, Handicapped Workers of America, started paying my tuition after that.

I started at the University of Tennessee-Nashville, which later merged with Tennessee State University. I began preparing a whole semester ahead of time. I went to the professors who were going to be teaching the courses I planned to take, found out what books they were going to be using, and made sure they weren't going to change them. Then I would go to the bookstore and buy those books and send them off to a place called Recording for the Blind in Princeton, New Jersey, and have those books put on tape. That's how I did my reading for class. I didn't even think to tell the administration that I was blind. I dealt with my professors more. They knew it up front, because sighted students could not bring tape recorders to class.

Before each semester started, I went to the school and found out what classroom my classes were going to be taught in and I started getting landmarks. I figured out, for example, when I got off the bus I would be right across from *this* building, so I'd just walk across and get on *that* sidewalk. The first time, I asked someone personally, "Where is the political science building?" So I would go where I thought they were pointing and then I'd ask again. I'd get to the next building for the next class, and anybody

I heard, I'd ask, "Am I in the math building?", and they'd say, "No, you've got to go next door", or "Yes, you're in the right building." Once I was in the right building, I would find classroom 107 or 215 or whatever. So I'd say to myself "top of the steps and then three doors on the right". So go to the top of the steps and count the doors. That's the way I did it the whole time. And I learned that stuff so that when school started, I walked the same path, and no one ever knew I was blind.

I couldn't see the names on the buses that I needed to take to get to campus. If someone was standing at the bus stop, I would ask, "Can you tell me when the Jefferson Street bus is here?" And as long as their own bus didn't come, they'd do it. But if their bus came, I'd have to find whoever was around next to tell me what bus was coming up. At the time, I guess they had the name at the top of the bus on a sign. I could never see that. But I knew what time the bus was supposed to be there. Sometimes, I thought it was the Jefferson Street bus, and I got on that thing, but I could tell by the turns it made, that it was not the right bus! So I would pull the chain, get off, and go back to the starting point. And by that time, I'd maybe missed the Jefferson Street bus.

Sometimes, I would get to school wet, because when you're blind, you want at least one of your hands free. I wasn't good at carrying a book satchel *and* an umbrella, because that left me vulnerable. As long as I kept one arm free, I could feel things when I was about to walk into them. I could reach out and block myself. To this day, I won't carry an umbrella; I don't care how hard it's raining. And I don't wear anything over my ears because I need my ears to see.

I didn't know to be scared. That's the way my life has always been geared. Do what I have to do to achieve this goal.

I would go home at the end of the day and, to solidify everything in my mind, I would transcribe the notes from these tapes onto my typewriter. I wasn't naturally smart. I had to go over stuff a *lot*. I paid people to read my notes to me and to come over and help me prepare for tests. I would pay five dollars an hour for that. My professors read my exams to me. (You're under a lot of pressure when your professor is reading the exam to you—you've got to know what you're talking about!) But the professors there were very, very helpful. Very compassionate, empathetic, and sympathetic. They bent over backwards to see that

I got what I needed. I still talk to some of them, even today.

There were kids who were so intelligent, they would be standing outside the door skimming the pages before a test, and they'd come out of the class with straight A's. Shoot ... every "A" I got required long hours of studying.

My demeanor was always, "I can deal with this. It's not going to do me in. I will deal with it." I was never one to wear my emotions on my sleeve. You could not make me cry. You could not discourage me to the degree that I would give up on things. You couldn't do it. It wasn't in me to quit. So if someone were mean or demeaning, if someone was trying to make me quit, it was never going to do that to me. I had lived through enough of that with my father growing up, so these insults didn't have any effect on me.

I am crediting my father for being the reason that I am how I am. He didn't know that, though. I'm sure he didn't set out to make me stronger. That's why I keep telling everybody, "I think God knows what He's doing." Without being sanctimonious or religious, that's the only thing I can attribute it to. I know that

I would be different if I were born to a different set of parents, or if I had been born with 20/20 vision.

I think without my father knowing what he was doing, he had that effect on me. The effect he had on my siblings was to let them know that they had to work. They learned that you have to work for anything you're going to get out of this life because he let us know from day one that he wasn't giving us anything.

Even my brothers who quit school in fourth grade worked right up until they died. I have a sister who worked until she was sixty-five, and she's just now learning to read. I have one brother who finished eleventh grade and went into the military. He fought in Vietnam and lived in Detroit for a long time, working in the automobile industry. My brother who I'm closest in age to has worked for almost forty years for the department of electricity where he lives, and he's caught pure hell on that job. He would tell me how other workers would come and say, "Joe, how many names do you people have? Nigger, jiggerboo, porch monkey…" And he'd just say, "I don't know." They treated him so poorly there, but he withstood that type of demeaning behavior because work was so important. He went through that the whole time he was there. It's probably eased up by now, but he hasn't forgotten it. Our emotional and psychological fortitude, the way our daddy brought us through, we could handle it. Because it was not an option to quit a job. Having a job was more important than anything.

Because work is the thing that sets you free.

CHAPTER TEN

Ramona

When I was going to school at night, I met my wife.

UT-Nashville used to be just one big building. This lady came in one night through the front door. I was waiting on a ride. She wanted to know where some place was—don't ask me how I knew where it was—I'd probably gotten lost in it sometime!

So I showed her. Then I saw her again; this time I was on my way to study for a test, and she asked if she could walk with me.

I couldn't see. I didn't know what color her hair was, what color her skin was, or what clothes she wore, but I could tell she was the prettiest thing that was ever at that school. And she was thirty times smarter than me. She was a medical student at the time, and she already had a teaching degree.

We started dating, and she may have thought I couldn't afford a car because she had to pick me up. Then I remember one date we were talking about high school, and I said I had graduated from the school for the blind. And she said, "What's that?" And I explained. Her response was, "But you're not blind!" She had never known it. I guess that's because I'm real slow and deliberate until I learn my path, but once I learn my way, I forget about being blind myself.

We used to go on dates to Montgomery Bell State Park. She liked to fish. I couldn't stand it. Everybody talks about how relaxing fishing is, and it drives me crazy! She liked to go out to eat, and she liked zoos and museums. It was a good experience for me because I hadn't been to a zoo in my life, or a museum. And she read a lot. She loved to read.

I remember meeting her parents for the first time. Her mother was quiet. She was very regal and serene. Her father was a retired Air Force man. Now, *he* was talkative. I don't know whether he ever really liked me or not. I could never tell—he just talked, talked, talked.

I was nervous meeting them. She's their only child. I think that they thought, *Well, if this is what she wants, we'll find out.* I never knew what they thought of me really, until one day when her mother said to me, "My daughter has found a great man."

She was the first girl I'd ever really dated, and I was in my twenties. But I could tell she was the right one for me by the way she was acting. She wasn't loud. She was extremely intelligent. She spoke calmly and softly. I knew she would always do what was right, and that's what I was looking for. I didn't have to worry about her. She wasn't going to be a wife or girlfriend that I was going to have to raise. She was already *there*. Marrying her was probably the most strategic decision I ever made. I don't *ever* worry about anything. She's her own woman. She's got her own head and she knows how to use it. She's like me, but in a softer way. I am an extreme pragmatist and she softens that. I can be hard. I can be like my father without the alcoholism, "This is what needs to be done; let's get it done." She helps soften that a lot.

For her, she didn't say it was love at first sight. She just said, "You were so nice, and so helpful, you seemed to be your own man. You didn't have a bunch of hoodlums around you. You came and went and did your thing. That's when I knew that you were the one for me." I think she really liked me and wanted to spend her life with me because of what I am: a pragmatist. She knew that I would never do anything stupid. I'd never go off on a tangent. I pretty much calculate everything. If something's not good for the whole family or society, I'm not going to do that thing.

CHAPTER ELEVEN

GE is Where I Want to Be

I had my own apartment, was dating Ramona, and was taking classes at UT-Nashville while working at AutoMart. I heard that General Electric (GE) in Hendersonville (located just north of Nashville) was hiring. I said to myself, "I'm going to try and get this job."

I called Harry Patterson, who was head of GE's Personnel Department, and he was really worried about hiring a blind person. He didn't want to do it. I would call once every other week, and he'd say, "Mr. Bailey, we just don't know. We haven't done it before." Then I started calling once a week. One time I called and he told me, "I'm going to meet with some people tomorrow. Give me a call tomorrow." I got anxious after that call. I didn't know what he was going to say.

I called back the next day around eleven in the morning and he said, "I talked to some people in manufacturing. Can you come in for an interview?" And I said, "Sure!" I thought that he was going to say, "Can you come in for an interview *this week*?" But he said, "Well, be here at one o'clock."

I didn't know how I was going to get to the interview, but I knew that I was going to get there even if I had to walk. I ended up taking a cab from Nashville to Hendersonville. When I got there, the cab driver let me out and said, "Okay, when you go up the sidewalk, you got about three steps and then you're on the porch, and just stay straight. The door's right in front of you." So I got out of the cab and walked right on up.

When I walk into a building, unless I hear something, I will kind of just stand there for a second or two until I get my bearings to see what I can pick up with my ears. The receptionist didn't say anything right away, she may have been working on something. And I didn't either—because I couldn't see her. Finally, she said, "May I help you?" And I said, "I'm here to see Harry Patterson." He was standing off to the side, and he said, "Well, Fred, you came through that gate well." I thought to myself, *I didn't know there was a gate. What gate?*

I had already told him by this point that I would work for two weeks for nothing just to show that I could do it, but he said that Tennessee labor laws wouldn't allow it. So they hired me, and I left UT-Nashville. I didn't even drop out, I just stopped showing up. I thought, "Forget that! GE is where I want to be."

I told Ramona that I was moving to Hendersonville, and she said, "I'm going with you." And I said, "Well let's find out who the judge is, and let's get this done."

We were married at the courthouse. Having the money to do other things was a lot more important than spending three or four thousand dollars on a wedding— forget all that nonsense. I am not a romantic man at all. I am an extreme pragmatist.

Harry Patterson later told me he followed me around for almost a month without my knowing, just to see how I would do. He said I became one of the best employees they had. I worked in the commercial industrial motor division—the guts of the motor before all the stuff goes into it.

So my persistence paid off in getting me the job of my dreams, but it turned out it wasn't meant to last a lifetime.

A Conduit for God's Plan

Harry Patterson was Director of Personnel for General Electric when Fred Bailey was applying for work there in 1977. These are his recollections.

When I think back on it, I could have lost my job. If Freddy had had an accident in the plant and there had been a lawsuit, they would have said, "Why in the world did you ever put that man in the plant anyway?"

But I'm convinced that God has a plan for everybody. I don't take any of the credit—I look at myself as a conduit for God's plan.

I started with General Electric in Rome, Georgia in 1953. I went from there to Phoenix, Arizona, and then to Hendersonville, Tennessee.

Originally, I started in the finance department when I was still going to school at night. I always wanted to get into personnel work, but was told I wasn't qualified. Then GE got in a bind to hire a bunch of people in a short period of time—this was when the computer was taking a lot of drudgery out of work—so they assigned me to personnel for six months, and then the guy I was working for got a promotion, and I got his job.

Back then, all industries had to have an affirmative action program. We had to write a very detailed plan and had to keep statistics on all of our employment, how many minorities we hired, what positions in the organization they held, what we were doing to recruit minorities, and all of that. GE had a strong plan.

I was in charge of affirmative action at the Hendersonville plant, and this man called on me from the state. He was with one of these agencies that help the handicapped and those who are released from prison to find employment. He said he had a couple of people he wished we'd consider for hiring. There was one white and one black. The black guy was Freddy, and the white guy had just gotten out of prison—he had been convicted of embezzlement at a bank. We interviewed both of them—and hired them both.

Freddy was always aggressive; he always wanted to do more and learn more. He wanted to know what I could do to help him advance.

He was on the second shift, and I used to worry about him getting to and from work. He had to walk four miles each way. He would walk to work down a busy road, staying off to the side where he could feel the edge of the pavement. And he was *never* late. Sometimes, one of the employees would offer to take him home at night. But if no one volunteered, he had to walk home. And this was second shift, walking home at eleven o'clock at night.

When I think back, there were a lot of coincidences that led to him being hired. For example, when we started the plant, you had to go through a pre-employment training program at the Hartsville, Tennessee, location before we would hire you. By the time Freddy interviewed, we had suspended that part of it because we were only hiring two or three people at a time as replacements or adding a few as business improved. If Freddy had come earlier, we would have never hired him because he would have had no way to get to Hartsville for the training. Then, not too long after Freddy arrived, I was moved to offices down near Rivergate (several miles away), so I didn't have further contact with him.

So timing was a factor. There had to be a master plan or something.

CHAPTER TWELVE

Freedom Comes in a Lot of Different Forms

I'd been working for GE for three years when they started laying people off. I thought it was probably just a downturn in the economy. I was laid off for about six months.

But then three or four years later it happened again, and I realized that I wasn't going to be in this job for the rest of my life.

So I went back to school. UT-Nashville had been combined with Tennessee State University by this time. I had accumulated some college credit, but my grades had turned into F's because I had just walked out. But I was determined. My wife worked in Nashville as a teacher, and she drove me to the bus stop. I would get on the bus, go into downtown, and transfer to the Jefferson Street bus to get to campus.

While I was taking classes, I also started doing volunteer work. I used to be the liaison or middle man between the state and the visually impaired of Sumner County. I would gather the visually impaired once a month and make sure they had everything that they needed in terms of glasses, eye care, etc.

I also knew I had to find some other type of work that I could do without too much assistance. I was extremely independent, and I wanted something where I didn't have to depend on anybody, something that I could manage myself. There were a lot of "get rich quick" schemes back then, and a big craze in the late 70's and early 80's were these infomercials that said, "Buy real estate for no money down—then sell the house and be a millionaire!" Of course, it wasn't as easy as Carlton Sheets advertised, but it did get me thinking about real estate. I was going around and telling people, "If you see any 'For Rent' or 'For Sale' signs, let me know." I had some money saved from working at GE.

We came upon a house one time, and I had some people I knew describe it to me. The house needed to be painted and the yard was overgrown. This was the kind of house I wanted. Usually the owner lived out of town, was paying taxes on it, and the house was being hit by vandals. They'd almost give it to you just to keep from having to pay the taxes. Those are the kinds of things I was looking to buy.

I would fix these houses up with friends of mine to get them ready to rent. I could do my own patching and painting. I could feel the dry wall, so I could patch it and let it dry and know whether or not it was smooth. Of course, I don't know what my painting looked like!

It worked out really well, I would just collect rent and when something needed to be fixed, I would get somebody to fix it. That was easy.

My wife and I were always like this: We wanted to be out of debt before we were fifty years old so that nobody could have anything over us. I kept telling her, "You and I are going to do without. Let's get what the kids need—let's get them through college—and we're going to make do with very little." By the time we were forty-six, we had houses and no debt.

People will say, "What's wrong with debt?" Well, you can never, ever, live up to your full potential when someone has you. Freedom comes in a lot of different forms, and one of them is remaining debt-free. That's what real estate did for me. No matter what happens, I know that I will have a roof over my head because I own my house. I think everybody ought to own a home. It's a right of adulthood. I'm not talking about renting or living with anyone else.

Later on, GE called me back again and I told them that I didn't need to come back, but I asked if they would pay for my education. They said yes, because I had been a good employee. So I took them my transcript and showed it to them, and they paid for my tuition.

I had to work especially hard to undo those F's at TSU, but I graduated with a 3.86 GPA. I didn't march—I didn't want the pomp and circumstance—I just wanted to get out of there. I was probably thirty-four or thirty-five when I finally got out of college.

I think my mother kept my college graduation picture up on her mantel until she died. By the time I graduated, she was on dialysis and not in good health. She was tickled when I took that picture up there, though. I was at her house one day when some friends came by to visit her, and she pointed up at the photo and said, "That's my son up there." You could tell she was grinning from ear to ear.

CHAPTER THIRTEEN

Existing Vs. Surviving

Schwerner, Goodman, and Chaney. Those three young men lost their lives so that I could have a better one.

James Chaney was black and from Mississippi. Andrew Goodman and Michael Schwerner were white and from New York. They were young guys, in their twenties. They were working to register black voters in Mississippi. They were murdered and buried in an earthen dam down in Philadelphia, Mississippi, because they were speaking out about how blacks should have the right to vote, and they were killed for it. I think my mother gave me the newspaper article. She read it to me and said, "Never disrespect these boys."

What did she mean? She wanted me to carry myself in a way that let these boys know that their dying was not in vain. That it meant something. She wanted me to live in a way that said, "I know what you were doing. I know what you wanted for me, and I'm going to live up to it, because you made the ultimate sacrifice and that was your life."

No one can pay you any greater honor than to lose their life for you.

Those young men realized that the power was in your vote, not your color. That's how you're going to make changes in this country—voting. They didn't lose their lives for Fred Bailey, African-American. They lost their lives for Americans, and Fred Bailey just happened to be a black one.

There's just no way that I could do some of the things that I see people doing because of the sacrifices of those three guys and countless others. The stuff that I see in society, especially with black individuals, it's like they don't understand how they got to be where they are. They don't understand how many people laid down their lives, how many people suffered indignities, how many people were lynched, beaten, and locked up so that they can have the rights that they have. When you know somebody has done that for you, the least you can do is to live up to what they fought for. Be the best that you can be. Take advantage of every opportunity—and reach back and bring the ones behind you up to the level where you are. That's what they wanted.

Today, when individuals find out, "I really don't have to work hard to make it," they get lulled into a false sense of survival. Some people will say, "Well, being on welfare, *that's survival.*"

No, it's not. It's not survival. It's existing. They're two different concepts.

I like to think of social services as *artificial* survival—it's not real survival.

I think some of the social programs may have started out with good intentions, but had unintended consequences. Let's just take welfare, for example. I grew up in the 1960's where, if a woman was on welfare, no man could live with you. There were checks where they would come into public housing and look for men's clothing to see if you had a man staying there. To me, all that was doing was busting up families. All you did was tell black people that the family unit wasn't important. To me, that was controlling, dividing, and destroying. To me, that's what you were doing, because if these women had babies and the fathers could not be there if they received assistance, then you were encouraging the fathers *not* to be there. This is why we are where we are right now. I don't know if it was deliberate, but I know there should have been enough statistics and enough proof that they should have ended welfare and tried something different.

When people start getting too many handouts, when people start helping people too much and in the wrong way, things start happening to people's psyche that they don't even realize until it's done. Being hungry is not the worst thing that can happen to you. I believe that when you let somebody do more for you than you are willing to do for yourself, that's the worst thing that can happen to you. Then you pretty much *are* done. Then you get on the slippery slope to losing your identity. And when you become a statistic, you are in a world of trouble. Anything that takes away from you being self-sufficient, you being independent to the degree that you can be, will reduce you more and more until you become an automaton. You own nothing, you probably will never own anything, and you don't *think* you should own anything. You look to someone else or something else for your whole sustenance.

The full human condition that you started out with has been diminished to the degree that you are now something else. And when you get reduced to that— slavery probably wasn't as bad. Now, you're basically going through life through osmosis. You're not even being propelled through life by your own power. It's almost like you're in suspended animation—someone else has you and is pretty much controlling you.

You can get deterred easily now because the government will back you up. Today, the human condition is such that people feel like they don't have to do *anything*. I can go to this place up there, and they'll pay my light bill. I can go over here, and they'll give me four, five, six hundred dollars' worth of food stamps. Programs like subsidized housing, free medical care, etc., have made it so easy that you can lose yourself without even realizing what is happening. And once you're in that predicament for twenty or thirty years, you're pretty much stuck there.

Since about 1975, it's been so easy to opt out of *survival* and to buy into *existing* that people believe that existing is the right way, that *this* is your human condition. And it *is* a condition—but it is not the condition that humans were made for.

People will say, "Good grief, if the service is out there and there's no need of going without lights, going hungry, then why shouldn't I take advantage of it?" But, you have to be wary of anybody giving you anything. The physical game is easy to win, the mind game is hard—because you have to be aware of it all the time—you've got to be mindful and cognizant. That's why I won't allow anyone to do too much for me. It strips you of so much of your human condition—of your full humanity.

That's why I fear the government to the degree that I do. Back then, if we didn't do what we were supposed to do, we couldn't eat. So, I grew up understanding that there is nobody but *me*. I have to look after my own life. The government is not supposed to back me, that's not what the government exists for, in my opinion. And if I allow the government to back me in any kind of way, then I have just reduced myself to the degree that I may not be able to recover. I'm not anti-government, and I think the government has some things that it does that are necessary. But when it comes to the psychological and emotional growth of an individual, it is incumbent upon that individual to have a life.

Now, anything goes in this society. We have lost so much of the human condition. Women can go out on the street almost naked. Guys can wear their pants off their butts. If you get tired of your kids, give them to foster care. The human condition was nothing like that in the beginning. It was strongly family-oriented, hard-working and respectful. Self-sufficiency—*that* was the human condition. When the government started doing more, the human condition started to become less. The government has a purpose, but I don't know that it has a purpose in your schools, your homes, and so forth. The government is a poor substitute for a mother or a father. Back off from the government and do more under your own power.

There are times when people probably do need help. When my family needed help, we didn't get it. We did without. My mother would never have gone and stood in a social program line. When our lights got turned off, they were just off. We did what we had to do while there was daylight and we went to bed when it was dark. Our clothes weren't good. We didn't eat all the time. My house was inadequate, it didn't have indoor bathrooms or insulation, but we never thought the government should give us better housing. Our human condition required us to start preparing for the cold weather, start cutting wood, start canning anything we could.

I found out later that a lot of the people who made fun of us when we were going to school were already getting social services—things that we had never even heard of. Most of those people didn't achieve anywhere near what my family achieved, because my family had those two things that caused us to rise above a lot of people: work ethic and respect.

My brothers and sisters are *surviving*—not existing—because they still will work two jobs, three if necessary. They get a job and they never quit it. The blind ones work, the uneducated ones work. They survive. Just about all of them plant gardens now—they're still eating out of gardens.

My father and mother taught us that whatever we were lacking, we could do without until we did better. That kept our human condition strong. You may say that the "human condition" is the same thing as pride and dignity. That's part of it. A person with no pride is an empty individual. A person who can't be embarrassed is a person who can't be helped. Some people say, "Well, pride goes before the fall." But it's not if you fall, it's whether you have the gumption to pick yourself up again.

A lady once said to me, "I just cringe when I see a blind person walk into something." Well, we're *blind*, we're supposed to be walking into things! I'm not going to let you help me until I absolutely need it. And I don't mind asking for help, but I'm going to try to do it on my own first, because that's important for my psychological and emotional character. A person that will ask first, without trying on his own, has no drive.

You are your own limit. If you have a challenge, whether you're deaf or blind or whatever, there are things that you can and can't do. But the things that you feel you can't do, you need to do to the fullest limit. You have to satisfy yourself that you are a whole person, and the only way you can ever be a whole person is to push your abilities to the limits.

CHAPTER FOURTEEN

Pragmatism and Fatherhood

Ramona does a good job of making us work—making us mesh and come together—a lot better than I could. I'm more of a person who likes to be in command and in control, because that's what I grew up with. It's all I knew. But she does a good job of making that livable.

Ramona and I have six children. There are biological, adoptive, and foster children. We are blessed with five sons and a daughter. Their names are Kemp, Thomas, Kenneth, Antwon, Dashawn, and Michelle. We make absolutely no distinction whatsoever amongst the siblings as to their families of origin. They are all our children and are loved and respected the same. We are Mom and Pop to all of them. There is no "step-sibling, half-sibling, adopted sibling, or foster sibling."

Sometimes people will ask me, "Which of these children are yours?" The short answer is: They are all my children. Why anyone would need to know any more than that is beyond my understanding.

When our son, Antwon was born I wasn't nervous about becoming a dad. I was used to kids. My character was set so tight that I was ready for whatever came my way. So being a dad came naturally.

Taking care of Antwon was no different than taking care of my younger sisters. I picked him up and changed his diapers just like I did theirs. I was protective of him. I would never turn him loose.

Whenever we went to the mall or a store, I always held on to him. As far as I'm concerned, every parent should do that, but I did that because I couldn't see. My wife could see him, but I never wanted him to get away from me.

I remember his first bicycle. We bought it for him when he was no more than six or seven years old. It was still brand-new years later when we gave it away, because I would never allow him to ride it out of the yard! When we were outside, I didn't let him get out of earshot. I made him always talk to me. I think he had his driver's license before he was allowed to ride that bicycle. It may seem strange to give him a bicycle and then restrict him for safety's sake, but I have never owned a bicycle and I wanted him to have one. I made sure that all of our kids had bicycles.

We each accepted responsibility for making sure the family ran smoothly. I knew that we were both responsible but I was going to take the lead role in it. I didn't believe, "This is my wife's job, this is my job—this is her part"—I was in all of the parts. I wasn't going to see laundry building up and think it was somebody's else's responsibly to wash, or see dishes in the sink and think it was somebody's job to wash them. I was just going to get the work done. I knew that my wife would get the kids' food ready and drive them to and from school and all that because I couldn't drive them. But I assumed the responsibility to get them ready to be driven.

They followed my lead. I used to play football with them out in the front yard, and then all the kids in the neighborhood would come over. We had a basketball goal up. I used to have a buzzard-bell up over my goal so I would know where the rim was, and I used a ball with a bell in it so I could keep up with it. They were fascinated with that stuff.

Sports are a good tool to mold emotions and psychological minds of young people. I knew from my own experience that wrestling teaches discipline, work ethic and respect. It's difficult to respect a person who just pinned you. It's not easy to do that, because you want to slug him! But if you can learn to respect him, you're going to be okay. Three of our sons played football. Two of the boys played baseball. Three studied martial arts. One played basketball, but he was really just brainy. Antwon played football and both he and Dashawn wrestled. I was one of Antwon's wrestling coaches. He was a better wrestler than I was.

I'm pragmatic all the time. I am not an affectionate anything, and I'm probably not the most fun guy. My kids know for a fact that they are loved, but they know that it's my brand of love. They probably know that it's different than what they saw in their friends' parents They understood that I never was the hugging, petting type of person, but they know that I was always there for them, and I was always aware of how they were maturing.

I used to tell them all the time that my job as a parent is to raise them into adults that can contribute to society and not always be consumers. If you can love me when I'm doing that, then I am okay with it. But

I'm also okay if you can't, because I still have to do my job. That's just the way it is. I'll never go all to pieces because I don't think my child loves me. That's not my job to have him love me. If I were affectionate and emotional, I probably would be upset all the time.

I look at some of the parents today who complain about their children being too belligerent and saying that they don't know what to do, and that they just want their child to love them. Well, that's your problem. When you just want them to love you, then you can't really do your job. You have to do what's best for them and what's best for this society that they are going to be a part of.

I told my sons when they were growing up, "I don't want you to be perfect. I don't even know what that looks like. Something tells me that being perfect would be boring. What I'm looking for is for you to know that you are an American citizen. Do you understand what that entails? Can you fulfill it? That is my job, to help my kids fulfill that. If I can get them to understand that, then I will not have a policeman throwing them to the ground, and they will not be locked-up in some cage. They will understand that they are to go to work, they are to always work and to provide for themselves. And they are always to respect themselves and others.

One of my sons, Kenneth, is in Chicago. He works for the Chicago public school system as a guidance counselor after earning an Ed.S. degree from MTSU. There is no question that he deserves combat pay! Antwon is also in Chicago. He is a director of health clinics. He has a Master's in Public Health from DePaul University. Currently, he is enrolled in Columbia University's School of Social Work enhancing his LADC II credentials. He works on some non-profit boards to fight human trafficking and serves as the president of the board of directors of the Susie Brannon McJimpsey Center, Inc. My son Thomas graduated from the University of Pennsylvania and works as a lawyer. There were times when his grandmother thought he was going to be a preacher, but I knew he was going to become a lawyer. He gives back to the community not only as an attorney who does pro bono work, but also as one of the guardians of the legacy of the Susie Brannon McJimpsey Center, Inc. My son Kemp is in Madison, TN. He completed certifications dealing with aircraft and the aerospace industry. He's more reserved, quieter and more introspective.

Dashawn enrolled at TCAT in Nashville. He has expressed an interest in their dental program.

Michelle is a senior at Hendersonville High School. She is the youngest and my only daughter. She loves to sing and she is good at it. I enjoy listening to her sing. She sings a lot of songs but she says that she is most interested in opera. I can't wait to see the choices that she will ultimately make.

Raising children can be challenging, I will admit. They don't arrive with a "how to" manual and if they did, there can't possibly be a universal manual that will work for all kids. Still, I had to do my best to lead by example, instill in them my work ethic, and help to set their character. We don't have the right not to make positive contributions to society.

CHAPTER FIFTEEN

Respect and Work Ethic

The idea for Children Are People came to me when I was working at GE. I had come home from work one day and I was just coming through the house and the TV was on. As I caught a little bit about what they were talking about, I stopped.

They had several people on this panel. I remember Jesse Jackson being on it, and they were talking about why the Great Society and the War on Poverty programs didn't work. They were discussing why poor people were still having such hard times after all this money had been spent.

And as I was listening to the different panelists talk about the reasons for it—racism, bad neighborhoods, the break-down of the family unit, the schools, all manner of excuses—it just dawned on me:

I am a product of everything they just talked about.

I thought that all of those things *could be factors* and all those things *do exist*. But you can let those things prepare you rather than define you.

My father is the one who made those things prepare me rather than define me. So I had to wonder, *How did he do it? How did he make me what I am?*

First, he taught me and my siblings respect. He made us respect ourselves and others. It was, "Yes, sir" and "No, sir" to everybody, and if we didn't say it he would knock us down right then. Second, he taught us work ethic. He had us working by the time we could walk. If we could walk, we could pick up sticks for kindling. And that's what we did. We may not have been able to carry the whole bucket of water, but we could carry our little jug. So he taught us respect and work ethic— those are the two things.

As I got older, I understood what he was doing. He was molding my character.

I remember thinking, *If I can ever get to where I don't have to work a nine-to-five job, I'm going to work with young people to show them what it's going to take for them to be successful in America, and more specifically, in a democratic, capitalistic system. Because I know that without respect and work ethic, you're not going to make it in this system.*

I didn't know how to do it because I had never done anything like that. I had never *wanted* to be bothered with teaching a bunch of kids about how to act, how to talk, how to carry themselves. I never thought I was cut out for that, or that it was my cup of tea. But something just kept pushing me to it.

It was 2001 when I finally found time to do something. It started out just as a family thing at first. I had great nieces and nephews that just weren't making it like I thought they should. They lived in Gallatin, Tennessee, and we worked it out with the public housing authority there that they would let me use one of their rooms. So the first eleven kids were my relatives. But after a while they started saying, "Uncle Freddy, my friend wants to come." Next thing I knew, I had thirty kids attending.

At first it was mostly about academics, because that's where I thought the problem was. They were D and F students and they had no pride. It didn't bother them at all to be failing in school. They knew they were going to be promoted to the next grade anyway.

I did the full-court press to get them out of that; I focused on working with them on their homework. I tutored math, Spanish, anything that they needed. I can do a lot of math in my head. I would make them read the problems to me, and then I would say, "Okay, tell me how you're working it." Then they would explain how they were setting it up and I could follow what they were doing and help them.

We would read a lot. After we'd read a passage, I'd ask them, "What did you just read?" They'd say, "I don't know." So, I'd say, "Okay, let's read it again." I found out that their vocabulary was limited. When you live on the street or in public housing and all you hear is cursing and the names of drugs, your vocabulary is very limited. So we had dictionaries all over the place. It made me realize ... I really think that some kids were better off during segregation than integration. During segregation, you might have a black doctor or lawyer living across the street from you. Everybody was out in their yards, and a doctor might come out and talk to you about what he did that day and he would get his scalpel out and show you what it looked like, and you at least heard medical terminology. Or, you might hear a lawyer say, "I have to defend kids who've been falsely accused." So you at least heard those words and built your vocabulary. Now, the kids don't see those people in their neighborhoods. They have no one to aspire to be, no role models; because after racial integration, we went back to segregation, but this time based on socio-economic factors. So if you're poor, and you don't have an inner drive or don't know how to dream about something greater, then the integration movement may have hurt you.

Teaching kids to write is difficult. I know how kids are and I could tell by the amount of time that they put into their writing that it was sloppy. So I would say, "No. You're going to have to rewrite that! That is *too* sloppy. I can't even read it! This is not even legible!" They never knew I couldn't see it. What they turned in the second time may have been just as bad, but I got them to stop just throwing anything together.

A lot of them would cry because I would make them work. They'd say, "I don't like coming here!" I'd say, "That's fine. That means you have some emotion we can work with. If you didn't say anything, I wouldn't know if there was anything to work with."

What I found out was that their brains were fine. They could do chemistry, they could do algebra, they could read well. If they're taught, then they're capable of doing it. And we proved that. We got them up to 3.9 and 4.0 GPAs in six months. We got them back on track.

Once we got the homework out of the way, I would say, "All right, let's dream." The first time I said that they said, "What...you want us to go to sleep?" I had to explain, "No, I want you to think about what you want to be when you grow up. I want you to think about what kind of life you'd like to lead. What would make you satisfied in life? Have you seen a house you would like to live in? What kind of job would support you in getting that house? Who do you admire and why?" I wanted to get them thinking in that frame of mind because I knew I had to start molding their character.

I taught them to always say, "Yes, sir" and "No, sir." One of my little nieces cried, "But Uncle Freddy—I *know* you!" I was always telling them, "I need you to be focused when an adult comes into this classroom. You keep your mouth shut and you sit up straight and wait. Because that is what society is looking for."

Soon, the people in public housing wanted to make what I was doing a part of their housing program, but I didn't want to be part of a government program because when you're paid by the government, you're limited in what you can say and do. For example, teachers have to play to the whims of the school board because the school board doesn't like complaints. I can't do that, because I've got to get at these kids' problems and get their character set by any means necessary. I can't worry about being politically correct, and I can't have my hands tied.

So the public housing people kicked us out. We moved to R.T. Fisher, which is an alternative school in Sumner County for students who have been expelled from their home schools, and they let us use their cafeteria for about six months. And then our current building came open and former Gallatin Mayor Don Wright and Sumner County Executive Hank Thompson told us we could use this building as long as we wanted it. It's not really suitable for what we're doing, but at the time, it felt like someone had just built me a university—it's a lot better than where we were.

CHAPTER SIXTEEN

The Modern Child

About five or six hundred kids have been through Children Are People (CAP) now, and a lot of kids have been helped. But it's a lot different than when we first started. CAP was an experiment to begin with, and initially we focused on academics. But it's become apparent that a lack of character is where the problem is.

I found that laziness is the one thing that underprivileged individuals cannot have in their lives. If they're willing to work hard, to dig deeper, they're going to make it. It's that, coupled with respect. It has nothing to do with their mom or dad or teacher. It's about *them.*

I realized that students who go to these modern schools, who ride these modern buses, they've never realized how they came to do that. If it weren't for the veterans of wars, the people of the civil rights movement, there's no way they would be experiencing the things they are experiencing right now.

I have to help them get a perspective, so I make them research individuals who've paved the way for them. I make them sit down and write a letter of thanks and appreciation for the sacrifices these people have made. There's no greater honor than having somebody lay down their life for you. If the individuals are no longer alive, then they address it to their relatives. I want them to let somebody know that they understand the sacrifices that were made. I have to make them understand how they came to be where they are. I tell them, "Never let your minds go far from these people because they will keep you anchored to your work ethic, to your respect. They are the reason you can have the opportunities that you do."

That opens their eyes as they do the research. I don't let them use a computer to write their reports, I make them do it with pencil and paper. I won't let them turn just anything in. I expect them to turn in work that they are proud of, work that is worthy of who they are. If it isn't, then they re-do it.

It's harder today for these kids, because they've got so many distractions. They've got social media, cell phones, and all kinds of nonsense. So it's a constant driving and pushing with the modern child because you are fighting all of these conflicting messages, and it's easy for my message to get cloudy. But no one is going to convince me to change. When they go home, my message gets cloudy. When they come back here, they hear it again. But as they get older, it will start grabbing hold and staying on longer and longer until they're out of college and they start working and are on their own.

One of the other big problems with our kids is, wherever the center is in the brain for dreaming, it's dormant in them. They really do not dream. You've got to have aspirations in order to strive for something, in order to achieve. But if you ask, "What do you want to be when you grow up?" They'll say, "I don't know." Or some will say a fireman or a policeman. Or, "I want to fix hair." But they're not dreaming, they're just mimicking, parroting what they see around them. I tell them, "I need you to go within yourself and ask, 'What does your mind, your conscience, tell you that you have an aptitude or a predisposition for?'"

We do everything we can to help them broaden their horizons. They've been to the civil rights museums in Birmingham, Alabama, and Memphis, Tennessee. Fifty-five students went to Washington, D.C. They've been to visit different businesses here in town. We do everything we can do for them within the means of our finances and staff. We have volunteers from all different walks of life who come here and share information about their professions, and who mentor them.

For example, I have a young lady who says she wants to be a pediatrician. She's going into the ninth grade. I've got her a coach, Dr. Rundus. I do that for the ones who know what they want to do. I've got a little boy now—he wants to be a zoologist—he's known since he was in the fourth grade this is what he wants. I've got to figure out a way to get him into that now, because he's in the seventh grade. So we've got to get him to the zoo and let him talk to some people to see what he needs to be doing. Another student, Nyadow, lived in public housing and wanted to be a doctor. You're not supposed to aspire to be a doctor if you live in public housing, you're supposed to just bide your time. Or, if you *do* go to college, you're going to be a teacher or a social worker. But I started a medical class here, and Nyadow was enrolled in it. Now, she's in medical school.

There was another young man named Trey. He's six-foot-four. Weighed three hundred and ten pounds when his momma started bringing him to CAP. He was making straight D's and F's. The mother said, "Mr. Bailey, can you do anything with him?" And I said, "I don't know, let's see if we can figure out what his problem is." I knew that he was bullying people at his school. His teachers were scared of him. I told Trey, "I'm not some little frail teacher that you can tower over and intimidate. Don't do that here. You either want to be here or you don't. Now, if you're going to be here, you're going to do exactly what I tell you, or you and I are going to tear this place down." After two or three months, Trey was A/B honor roll. It never was his brain; it was his character.

Today, we focus almost ninety percent of our efforts on getting the kids' character set tight with those two main elements anchoring it: respect and work ethic. Those are the two things that are missing in America, and that is what Children Are People is all about. I'm not crazy about wearing dress shirts and ties all the time, but I do it to set an example for the kids. I want them to see that I'm black, I'm blind, and I look professional every day.

We're teaching these kids what America is looking for from them, because they are going to have to give what it requires. When they get their character set it also gets them ready for their real, true boss—life.

The thing I like about life is that it treats us all the same. Rich people get cancer just like poor people get cancer. Black people have car accidents just like white people have car accidents. Life says that your blackness, your whiteness, your blindness, your deafness is irrelevant. What drives you in life is your ability to adapt and adjust. If you can grasp that and get that under your belt, you're going to make it through.

I'm sixty-six years old and even when I thought my life was bad, it was only bad in relation to my inability to adapt and adjust. As soon as I learned to adapt and adjust, I was fine. That ability will set your character in cement. Now there are certain lines that I could never cross because of the way my character is set. I could never steal—not even if I'm starving. I could walk past a car with a million dollars lying on the seat and I could no more touch that million dollars than I could touch the moon. It's nothing about being sanctimonious or religious or spiritual. It's just the way my character is set.

You might say, "Well, you can't do it because you can't see it." But even if I got my vision back today, it would not alter my character from what it is now. It is an internal thing. And that's what we're trying to develop at CAP.

There's very little turnover here. The kids never leave until they graduate. When they're young, they come for the consistency. These young kids are used to their mothers changing boyfriends every six months. They move three or four times a year. Nothing is constant. They get used to that, so they don't trust anything. That's why when we first started this organization, these kids balked. I knew what they were doing—they were trying to run us off. They wanted to prove that we didn't care. But when they realized, "Good grief, Mr. Bailey is still here," they finally settled down and started to work. Now, they know that I'm in their building somewhere even if they don't see me. They feel comfortable with that. And that's another big part of it: security.

I talk hard to them. I'm always teaching them how to interact within a group of people, how to work together to make something work. How if something doesn't go their way, to keep moving and not fall to pieces, but instead learn to do it a different way next time. There is an agenda to everything.

For example, I like wrestling or playing football or basketball, but at CAP, sports have a purpose. I'm always watching and listening to see how the kids react when they think they got fouled too hard. If they don't react the way that I think they should, that's when the lesson comes in.

I've been coaching wrestling since high school. I've got mats in a warehouse and I work the CAP kids out in there. I also work with a mixed martial arts gym in Nashville. I don't ever take a break from it. I'm coaching somewhere all the time. I put in six to eight hours in a week.

I actually get down on the mats and work with the kids, show them the moves, so I can tell them what they're doing right and what they're doing wrong. I can tell how well they're doing when I'm down on the mat with them, but I couldn't if I were just walking around. I'm in pretty good shape—but six minutes is rough these days!

Whether they become wrestling champions is really not that important to me; I want them to become champions in life. Wrestling is a good tool to make that possible because you've got to be extremely disciplined in almost every aspect of your life to be really, really good at it. Wrestling, basketball, baseball, and football are nothing but tools to teach life skills. That's all they are to me. This child may be having a tough time picking up a work ethic and character in the classroom, but he actually can get it through a sport *if* the sport is taught on that foundation. But, if all a coach is thinking about is winning, you're going to lose that child. The child may go on to become a champion in the sport, but he may not be a champion in life. I'm always making sure that they get the necessary skills to adapt and adjust out here in life through that sport. If they can do that, they'll be very successful Americans.

Sports are a very, very small part of who you really are, or what you really are. I may be a wrestling champion, I may have an NBA ring—but did I maintain my character all the way through achieving the NBA ring or winning the first-place medal in the event? That's what you want because that makes the medal or the NBA ring all the more significant. But if I got that NBA ring or that state champion medal and I was trouble all the way through, then I have diminished it. That's what I look at when I coach.

I'm pushing these kids to aspire to something higher, to something greater. And there are a million more kids that need to come through here.

I Call Him the "Kid Whisperer"

Susan Superczynski is Director of Operations for Children Are People. She's been with the organization since 2007, and these are her insights.

When the buses arrive at CAP, the kindergarten through fifth grade students run, full-out. The little ones fall over each other to get into the building because they're so excited. We stand at the door and greet them, calling them by name. We compliment their outfit or hairstyle or their new shoes or *anything* to be personal. We want them to know, "I see you." Our teachers are doing the same thing—helping them with their homework and working on their manners.

The high schoolers are dragging when they get here, and the middle schoolers are a little more eager, but not running. They know they're going to get a hot meal; someone is going to talk to them and ask them how their day was. Most of these kids don't get that at home.

Mr. Bailey was talking to our middle school class one day, and he asked them, "What is your morning routine?" Half of them said they never see their parents. They get themselves up and dressed and on the school bus while their parents are sleeping. They come home and go to their rooms. Their parents may work third shifts, or there's alcohol or drug abuse. They're just not there—mentally or emotionally—for their kids.

I can remember the first time I saw Fred get in a child's face in a physical way. It shocked me because I didn't come from that world. In schools, you're not allowed to do that. But here he did it to get the child's attention. He knew what the child needed.

At the time I didn't have a full understanding of *his* understanding of the kids. But now I totally trust his intuition. I call him the "Kid Whisperer" because he can cut through all those layers of attitude and self-doubt and home life and street cred and whatever else you want to call it, to get to the core of what makes that child tick and what is inhibiting his or her progression into the future.

It's intrinsic for him—he doesn't even realize how gifted he is in that area. I've learned at his knee and I can execute some of it, but he has a connection with these children that I will never have. He just comes from such a place of love and they know that, so they listen. He gets through to them and they don't come back with, "I'm going to tell my mom and you're going to be in a lot of trouble." I've never heard anyone say that to Mr. Bailey.

He's in their corner. He's their father figure, he's their mentor. He's their hero. He's someone they aspire to be like. Mr. Bailey will do whatever it takes to get what he thinks these kids need.

I've opened a center in downtown Nashville. It's called the Susie Brannon McJimpsey Center, Inc., named after my mother-in-law. We're doing things differently at this center than when I started CAP. In Gallatin, I just jumped in and learned how to swim once I got in. Here, I built my staff first and I told them: these children are going to come to us already an emotional wreck. I don't care if they are quiet, and I don't care if they are making straight A's in school. The environment these kids are coming from is producing individuals without the human condition intact.

It has been a real eye-opener for me. Today, the urban child has seen more in nine years than I've seen in sixty-six. A lot of things that have happened to these kids has truly created a new psychosis—a pathology.

For example, an animal operates on instinct. It will kill for food, or to save its life, or to protect its young. And a human sometimes kills if provoked, or for protection or with reasoning—even if it's wrong. But what is it when a gang member will go to a park, where there are women and children, and start randomly shooting and killing people? It's a cross between a human and an animal, but it's neither. I've never seen anything like it. It kills on instinct—but not to eat, or to protect. And it's not provoked, or using reasoning. But this is what we're producing more and more of, out here in society. These kids now need some real medical attention—it's gotten to that. They haven't been treated as a human being, or even as well as an animal. And now, they can kill unprovoked—for no reason. That's a scary thing to me.

Downtown, we have a staff of fifteen, and they cover all strata of society. One wants to work on self-esteem, another wants to teach them how to cook and set tables; there's a retired medical doctor who's going to teach them about nutrients and physical health. We have a math major, a foreign language major, two retired teachers, a gentleman who does anger management, a lady who wants to do devotionals. And people who are going to teach tap, ballet, jazz, drums, theater, and chess.

If I'm not careful and if I'm not vigilant, these kids will go into existing rather than surviving. But if I can get them in a surviving mode, everything else will make sense.

CHAPTER SEVENTEEN

Something Else is Guiding Me

Early on, I didn't hear the name of God. I don't remember hearing anything about God, a Bible, a church, or a pastor. We lived so far out in the country that we never went to church.

When I was about nine or ten, we moved to another farm—the Hughes farm. I don't know why. This is where I was when they came to talk to me about the Tennessee School for the Blind. This farm was right on the road, with a few houses on up the way. It was on a dirt road, and trucks would come through with water in the summertime to wet it down so it wouldn't be so dusty. There was a little church diagonally down the street that my mother would go to, and a lot of my brothers and sisters were baptized there. I remember my Daddy went one time. He washed his face, put on his hat, and he put on a shirt and tie. He always wore these canvas shoes with rubber bottoms—I called them deck shoes. But Reverend Adams made a mistake. I believe his sermon that Sunday was on alcoholism, and Daddy never went back.

But church for me wasn't that building. Church for me wasn't in those pews. It was a *knowing*, that somebody or something is guiding me—because I don't have the wherewithal to be making these decisions.

The reason I know that something else is guiding me is that I just don't know that, on my own, I would stand out in the rain to catch a bus, then get on the wrong one, have to get off and go back to square one—then miss the bus altogether. And I don't know that I would have been able to walk four-and-a-half miles from my house to GE every day. I had to be at work by four o'clock and my wife was working in Nashville; she couldn't get back to Hendersonville in time to get me there. So I had to leave at two o'clock to start walking.

Even starting CAP. If you'd told me that I was going to be working with a bunch of hard-headed kids eighteen years ago, I'd have told you that you were crazy.

I don't know how God works. I truly don't. I just know that He does. With my reasoning, I wouldn't have done some of these things—shoot, no! A person can only take so much.

I feel like I'm being orchestrated; I feel like I'm being maneuvered. It's truly weird to me. I don't even like the way it sounds; it sounds so spiritual. For the last twenty or thirty years, I've felt like I'm being nudged, pushed, and eased to do these things. Why me? I couldn't tell you. But I'm living proof there is a God, because He's pushing me.

Do I pray? In my way, I do. When I walk outside, I just marvel sometimes. I especially like early mornings. I marvel at how nice it is, and I'll say something like, "God, gosh, how do you do this? What a day. How does it work?"

But I've never prayed for help for CAP. Here's what I've found out: whenever I think CAP is about to go out or go under, He puts the funds there. He knows exactly what CAP needs. So I don't ask Him for much, because I know He will have it available. As long as He wants CAP to go on, He will provide what it needs. When He doesn't, then it will be time for me to do something else. That's just the way I see it. We've been nickel-and-diming it for eighteen years. There's a whole lot of nonprofits that were more established and around many more years before we started that are gone now. He has some plan for these kids and for me. As long as He has that plan, we don't have to worry about it. We are here doing fundraisers and so forth, but CAP will get what it needs when it needs it.

CHAPTER EIGHTEEN

Don't Let Your Struggles Define You

Whatever you've been through, *or whatever you're going through*, don't let it define you. Instead, let it prepare you for what you're going to encounter in life.

I've been through it all. Physically abusive, alcoholic father. Being afraid of him and hiding in the woods, in the cold. No food to eat. Digging through the trash dump trying to find some. No way to take a bath. Shoes with no soles. Being made fun of and humiliated for being poor, for being black, for being blind. Being told, "No"—my *kind* wasn't welcome, wasn't hire-able.

Remember what my momma said: Anyone who tries to demean you is a fool, because you're as good as anybody. Push past those people. When someone tries to tear you down or stop you from being an achiever, you say to yourself, "That just made me stronger. I'll find another way. I'm going to persevere." It will be hard; you have to dig deep every day. But believe in yourself. Respect yourself. And respect everyone you encounter; you don't know what others have been through or are going through now.

If we lived in a country other than the United States of America, I might not be able to offer you hope. But remember, there are people from other countries literally dying just trying to get to America, every day. They come here with no money, no clothes, no food, no relatives, no friends. *Nothing*. And they are thankful to get here. Why? Because they know that, in the U.S., there's hope. They have a chance. If they're willing to treat others with respect and to work hard, they can build a new life. A good life. Even a great life. If you're in America, you already won the lottery. You have no idea how much worse life could be if you were living in an oppressive country. It is never too late to start working toward the life that you want. There are three keys that correlate with rising above a life of poverty. First, graduate from high school. Second: don't have children until you're married, and don't get married until you're financially independent and mature enough to handle it. And third, get a full-time job. Set your mind to do these three things, and never waiver. If you need to go back and get your GED because you didn't graduate high school, then do it. Then get a job, or two jobs or three jobs. Whatever it takes. Don't rely or wait on the government to make sure you have a good life; stand on your own power. It's your life and your choices. Your decisions. Your character.

For example, I never truly liked being at the Tennessee School for the Blind. I just never did. In fact, I used to tell myself that I was *going* to quit, every year. That's the only way I made it through. It got to the point where the authoritarian-type atmosphere just wasn't good in some cases. There was a dormitory supervisor there that was so mean and hateful; I just got tired of it. I remember talking to Coach Brewer one time, and he said, "You don't want to quit, because you don't have a future without an education." So I hung in there that year. But I kept saying I was going to quit every year until I graduated because that was the only way, mentally, that I was able to stay there.

At the same time, by the time that I got to the age where I could discern things, that I could reason, I realized this school was the best place for me. I became a true pragmatist without even knowing what it meant. I knew what was beneficial to me, and I made the best of it, whether I liked it or not. If it was going to benefit me, I endured whatever. I was in a class with people that were smarter than me, and I had to work at my grades—I had to dig for A's and B's. I hadn't been exposed to anything—things I learned at age sixteen, I should have known at age nine. But whatever situation I was in, I was going to adapt and adjust to it until I could get to the next phase.

At Children Are People, our students come from the drug-infested projects, living in dire poverty, neglect and abuse, yet they rise above their circumstances. They go to college, the military, even medical school. And it isn't just a few who escape the lives they're born into, it's every single one who decides to follow those three keys and to do whatever it takes. You can, too.

Work hard for the life you want. It will be worth it.

ACKNOWLEDGEMENTS

I thank everyone who encouraged me to share my life story and publish this book, and who continues to support our efforts to offer disadvantaged young people a chance at defying the odds. A special thank you to Harry Patterson, Ralph Brewer, and Susan Superczynski for being interviewed and sharing their remembrances of time spent with me, and also to Susan for her ideas on the book cover. My appreciation to Morgan Myers for her photography assistance, and to Amanda Varian for the photography on the back cover; to Rebecca Lunsford and Rory J. Thompson for their editorial input and proofreading; to my wife, Ramona, for reading the manuscript to me multiple times and helping me with all of the back-and-forth communication; to Rick Isaacson for his ongoing support and encouragement; and to Susan

White Newell, for time spent interviewing me and transforming my stories into a book that captures both my life story and my message of hope for others, and posthumously to her mother, Elizabeth White, who also supported this project and my mission.

ABOUT THE AUTHOR

Fred Bailey is the founder of two nonprofit organizations in the Greater Nashville area, both of which are focused on building the character and self-esteem of children from disadvantaged backgrounds. His goal is to empower others to champion their own lives and achieve their full human potential. He uses his own life as a teaching tool—having overcome multiple forms of adversity himself, including abject poverty, blindness, and discrimination. His philosophy is simple: hardships can either confine you, or they can be leveraged as preparation for the obstacles and hurdles everyone encounters at some point in life.

FRED'S NUMEROUS ACCOMPLISHMENTS AND AWARDS INCLUDE:

- First Runner-Up, Tennessee State Wrestling Tournament, 1969
- Graduate, Tennessee School for the Blind, Donelson, TN – 1975
- Employed, General Electric (commercial and industrial motor division), Hendersonville, TN. 1977–1985
- Graduate with honors, Tennessee State University, Nashville. Bachelor of Science (Political Science/Pre Law) – 1989
- Self-employed real estate entrepreneur, early 1980's – present
- Founder and executive director of Children Are People (CAP), a nonprofit after-school program for disadvantaged youth in Gallatin, TN. 2001–2018
- Founder and executive director of the Susie Brannon McJimpsey Center, Nashville, TN, a nonprofit offering summer and holiday programming for disadvantaged youth. 2014-present
- Founder of the Tennessee Association for Visually Impaired Athletes, and of support groups for blind and visually impaired residents in Sumner County, TN. Volunteer youth wrestling coach for the past thirty-plus years.
- Recipient of a 2014 Jefferson Award for the state of Tennessee. The Jefferson Award is the nation's longest-standing public service honor, co-founded in 1972 by Jacqueline Kennedy Onassis, U.S. Senator Robert Taft, Jr., and philanthropist Sam Beard.

- Numerous awards and proclamations from Tennessee governors, the TN Senate and House of Representatives, the Tennessee Education Association, the Nashville Business Journal, the Greater Nashville Alliance of Black School Educators, local mayors, and regional chapters of national service organizations.